BECAUSE THEY MARCHED

BECAUSE THEY MARCHED

MARCHED

*The People's Campaign for Voting Rights
That Changed America*

RUSSELL FREEDMAN

Holiday House / *New York*

Picture credits appear on page 79.

HOLIDAY HOUSE is registered in the U.S. Patent and Trademark Office.
Printed and Bound in April 2014 at Tien Wah Press, Johor Bahru, Johor, Malaysia.
www.holidayhouse.com
First Edition
1 3 5 7 9 10 8 6 4 2

Library of Congress Cataloging-in-Publication Data
Freedman, Russell.
Because they marched : the people's campaign for voting rights that changed America / Russell Freedman. — First edition.
pages cm
Includes bibliographical references and index.
ISBN 978-0-8234-2921-9 (hardcover)
1. Selma to Montgomery Rights March (1965 : Selma, Ala.)—Juvenile literature.
2. Selma (Ala.)—Race relations—Juvenile literature. 3. African Americans—Civil rights—Alabama—Selma—History—
20th century—Juvenile literature. 4. African Americans—Suffrage—Alabama—Selma—History—20th century—Juvenile literature.
5. Civil rights movements—Alabama—Selma—History—20th century—Juvenile literature. I. Title.
F334.S4F74 2014
323.1196'073076145—dc23
2013038991

To Dick and Joan Bahm

Friends from the beginning

The Great Alabama Freedom March: Moving through a steady rain, voting rights marchers approach the midway point on their 54-mile trek from Selma to the state capitol in Montgomery, March 23, 1965.

Dr. King used to say there is nothing more powerful than the rhythm of marching feet, and that was what this was, the marching feet of a determined people. That was the only sound you could hear.

John Lewis, *Walking With the Wind*

CONTENTS

African Americans line up to register as voters at the Dallas County Courthouse during the 1965 Selma, Alabama, voting rights campaign. The line stretched for five blocks that day.

One

The Day the Teachers Marched

Dressed in their Sunday best—women in high heels and white gloves, men in suits wearing tie clasps—they might have been on their way to church. But on this particular Friday afternoon, January 22, 1965, Selma's black schoolteachers were about to risk their jobs, their freedom, and their personal safety. They were headed for the county courthouse, where they would demand their right to register as voters.

For months the small city of Selma, Alabama, had been the scene of mass meetings, protest marches, arrests, and violent confrontations between black voting rights demonstrators and white law enforcement officers. A local judge had issued a court order putting an end to the demonstrations, and for a time the city was quiet. But Selma's black community would not be silenced. When the local court order was appealed to a federal court, voting rights demonstrators took to the streets again.

Until now, the city's black teachers had not taken part in the protests. They had to answer to a school board made up entirely of whites. If arrested, they could lose their teaching positions and their hard-earned advantages of security and respect. So the teachers had stood aside and watched as others fought for voting rights. But on this day, to the surprise of almost everyone, 105 teachers from Selma's all-black segregated schools were making their way along the city's streets toward the Dallas County Courthouse in the center of town.

Because protest marches had been banned, the teachers were careful to avoid any impression that they were in fact *marching*. Instead, they *walked* two abreast along the sidewalk, not bunching up but keeping a

Frederick Douglass Reese, president of Selma's black teachers association, led the teachers' march for voting rights.

wide space between pairs, as though they were out for a casual afternoon stroll. Leading the procession was the Reverend Frederick Douglass Reese, himself a schoolteacher. "How can you teach citizenship," Reese had asked, "telling boys and girls to be good citizens and you are not registered [as voters], and you are making no attempt to register?"

As the teachers passed the George Washington Carver houses, a housing project for poor black families, people came out of their homes to encourage them. "Students who were home from school by this time cheered with delight," Reese later recalled. "Black mothers held their babies and watched with great satisfaction as we marched toward the courthouse." Some folks tagged along at a distance and followed the procession into the heart of town.

In Selma's business district, white merchants came out of their stores and watched in silence. "You pay for everything you get in those stores," Reese called out to the marchers. "Don't worry about a thing. Keep moving."

Across from city hall, a black reporter waiting in a phone booth spotted the approaching procession. He grabbed the phone, dialed his editor, and shouted, "I can't believe it! This is bigger than [President] Lyndon Johnson coming to town!"

When the teachers reached the courthouse, those in front of the procession climbed the marble steps to the entrance. The chairman of the school board, E. A. Stewart, and the superintendent of schools, J. A. Pickard, were waiting for them. They urged the teachers to turn around and leave, warning them not to make an "illegal attempt" to enter the courthouse. "If you do, you are in danger of losing all the gains you have made," Stewart threatened them.

Reese explained that the teachers had asked the board of registrars to set aside a day each week for employees of the public schools to register as voters. The board had refused. "You cannot come in here and register now," Stewart replied. "The board is not open."

"We want to see for ourselves if the board is open," Reese said. He had known all along that the registration office would be closed. Normally it was open just two days a month, and then only for a few hours. The teachers' plan was to show how difficult it was to register, by marching past the closed door of the registration office and then out of the building.

"Dr. Reese, you have made your point," Stewart said. "Take the teachers home."

"We have the right to enter our courthouse," Reese replied.

Sheriff Jim Clark, "a stern-faced man who weighs 220 pounds," as a reporter described him, stood blocking the courthouse door. He was flanked by volunteer deputies. They had no official uniforms, but wore helmets of various kinds from army surplus stores, motorcycle shops, and hard-hat construction sites, each bearing a small silver decal with "Sheriff's posse" spelled out in black letters. They held heavy wooden nightsticks and had revolvers strapped to their waists. Some carried cattle prods that could deliver a painful electric shock without leaving a telltale mark. Across the street a crowd of reporters, photographers, and TV cameramen from all over the country watched the tense scene as they stood clustered behind a police barrier.

Sheriff Clark fingered the nightclub that dangled on a strap from his wrist. "You can't make a playhouse out of the corridors of this courthouse," he told Reese. "Some of you think you can make it a Disneyland. I'll give you one minute to clear the steps."

When the teachers refused to move, the sheriff drew back and began to jab Reese in the ribs with his nightstick. "The deputies immediately imitated the sheriff's behavior," Reese recalled. "They began jabbing other teachers and wildly pushed us down the courthouse steps. We began to fall back like bowling pins.... Our supporters from the projects who had followed us were getting an eyeful."

So were the reporters, photographers, and cameramen who were recording the confrontation from across the street.

Teachers gasped for breath, doubled over in pain, fell to the steps. Within minutes Clark and his deputies had cleared the courthouse steps from top to bottom. "We are going back up," Reese yelled. "Like a military commander in battle, I turned and shouted to the marchers, 'Rrrreeeggroup!'

"No coaxing was necessary.... The teachers regrouped and we went up the steps in double file, each person staying with his or her original partner, and waited to be admitted inside.... Once more the sheriff and his deputies started jabbing us with their clubs and pushed us back down the steps. The teachers went up the third time at my order. Once we were in place, the sheriff said, 'Leave in one minute or get arrested.' "

The two men stood facing each other as Sheriff Clark ticked off the seconds. Then the glass door to the courthouse swung open and Clark was summoned inside. When he came out a few minutes later, he and his deputies began jabbing with their nightsticks again, forcing the teachers back down the steps.

"I knew [now] that we were not going to be arrested," Reese said. "If we were going to be arrested, the sheriff would have signaled his men as soon as he came outside.... The white folks knew these teachers had influence, and to arrest them would have been a crucial mistake. Though we did not get inside the courthouse, we made our point. The teachers had no regrets."

Back on the sidewalk, the teachers reassembled. Then they turned around and marched two abreast to Brown Chapel African Methodist Episcopal Church, where a waiting crowd of students cheered and applauded. "The march turned into a parade," said Reese. "The scarred and aching teachers received a hero's welcome."

The teachers' march that day would be remembered as a turning point in the struggle for equal voting rights. For the first time, a recognized professional group from Selma's black community had carried out an organized protest.

By demonstrating in defiance of their white employers, the teachers had acted with courage. Yet they were following in the footsteps of their students. Selma's black teenagers had been marching, protesting, and submitting to arrests for months. They had taken their lessons in citizenship and civic responsibility to heart, setting an example for their teachers.

Sheriff Jim Clark points a billy club and, beneath the club, an electric cattle prod at a voting rights demonstrator on the steps of the Dallas County Courthouse.

Two

"White Folks' Business"

In Alabama and across the South during the early 1960s, African Americans were denied the most fundamental right in a democracy—the right to vote. Selma, a former slave-trading town and the Dallas County seat, had 15,000 blacks of voting age, but only 335 were registered to vote. That compared to 9,300 registered voters among 14,000 eligible whites.

The Fifteenth Amendment to the Constitution, approved in 1870 after the Civil War, states that the right of U.S. citizens to vote "shall not be denied or abridged by the United States or by any State on account of race, color, or previous condition of servitude." Even so, Selma's white voting registrars rejected most black applicants. As a result, few blacks even tried to register, and the local government remained securely in white hands. Voting, as some blacks liked to say, was strictly "white folks' business."

One barrier facing potential voters was the poll tax, a special tax required of all voters that many blacks and poor whites could not afford to pay. Limited registration days presented another obstacle. In Selma the voter registration office was open for just a few hours on two Mondays a month. Black applicants who had taken time off from work might be kept waiting in line all day until the office closed, only to be told to come back some other time.

Applicants who were admitted to the office had to take a written literacy test. If they failed to dot an *i* or cross a *t*, they could be rejected. Those who passed the written test took an oral exam that was rigged to disqualify even the most highly educated blacks.

A young demonstrator with "VOTE" stenciled on his forehead in white paint.

A masked Ku Klux Klansman displays a hangman's noose as a warning during a drive through a black neighborhood the night before an election, Miami, Florida, May 3, 1939.

"The written test was only part of the reason for concern," lamented Ernest Doyle, a black college graduate and veteran of World War II. "The verbal questions the registrar asked that were not on the written test made passing nearly impossible." One question put to him was "How many bubbles are there in a bar of soap?" Of course, he said, "Any answer you gave was wrong."

The biggest barrier to voting, however, was the fear of reprisals. For an African American living in the Deep South in the 1960s, voting was not just a forbidden act, it was a dangerous act. "Black people in Selma were hesitant about getting involved [in politics]," Bernice Morton, a longtime Selma resident and voting rights activist, recalled. "[They] were afraid for their safety or their jobs."

When a local black minister, J. D. Hunter, brushed aside warnings to stay out of politics, segregationists burned his house to the ground. "That fire went out," Mrs. Morton said, "but the fire that was burning inside of the preacher could not be quenched."

Ernest Doyle not only flunked the bubble test, he almost lost his carpentry business. "They boycotted my business because of my political activities," he said. "White people were encouraged not to use or hire me to do any work. Business fell off. I felt the economic squeeze in my pocket, but I felt another squeeze in my heart."

Members of the Ku Klux Klan and other white supremacy groups did not shrink from violence. In 1964 near the town of Philadelphia, Mississippi, three young civil rights workers—two white, one black—were killed by a mob of Klansmen for helping local blacks register as voters.

Back then, racial segregation was strictly enforced throughout the South. "Jim Crow" laws, dating to the Reconstruction period following the Civil War, upheld white supremacy and kept blacks in their place as second-class citizens. Blacks were born in separate hospitals, attended separate schools, worshipped in separate churches, and were buried in separate cemeteries. They rode in the back of public buses, sat in the balconies of segregated movie theaters, and swam at segregated beaches.

"When I was twelve or thirteen, I'd go to Newberry's with friends," remembered Larry Russell, who grew up in Birmingham, Alabama. "They had one water fountain for whites, and one for us. I used to think, What's the difference between colored water and white water? What does white water taste like?" He decided to find out.

One evening as the store was closing, Larry and a friend managed to sneak a sip from the white fountain. "It tasted no different. Water was water." The only difference was the mechanism—how the water was delivered. "With the black one," he said, "you practically had to put your mouth on the thing to drink out of it. On the white side they hardly had to bend over. Their water came up so free. This was mystifying."

Annie Lee Wilkerson Cooper, who grew up in Selma, remembered when "Drinking fountains were still segregated, as well as restaurants.... There was a local Dairy Queen, but black customers had to go to a window on the side to be served. White customers went to the main window at the front."

Segregated drinking fountains labeled "WHITE" and "COLORED" in the Dougherty County Courthouse, Albany, Georgia.

In Evergreen, Alabama, Jerome Gray, still living across the street from the segregated high school he attended in the 1950s, remembered when the movie theater was segregated too: "You had to go down an alley and up the stairs" to a balcony reserved for blacks. "We called it the buzzard's nest.... We had no elected black officials anywhere. [To vote], blacks had to get a written statement from a white business-man to say they were 'a good Negro.' "

Barred from the ballot box, Southern blacks had no say in electing government officials, no voice in influencing the laws that kept them separate and apart. But as the song said, the times, they were a-changin'. And as the pace of change accelerated, the voices of protest grew louder and demanded to be heard.

As black servicemen returned to the South after World War II, they began to ask why they should be oppressed at home when they had fought (in segregated combat units) to liberate people in distant lands. In Selma, black war veterans joined the all-black Dallas County Voters League, which introduced a literacy program and urged blacks to register as voters. The league also called for the integration of the county's schools. "We drew up a petition and presented it to the local board of education," Ernest Doyle recalled. But the board never replied. Most signers of the petition "had to leave town because of intimida-tion and the economic squeeze the white people put on them."

Elsewhere in the South, the struggle for equal rights was moving into the federal courts and, increas-ingly, into the streets. In a momentous 1954 court case called *Brown v. Board of Education*, the U.S. Supreme Court ruled unanimously that segregation of the nation's public schools violated the constitutional rights of black students—a landmark decision that would affect race relations across America.

A year later in Alabama's capital city, Montgomery, Rosa Parks refused to surrender her seat to a white man and move to the back of a city bus. Her quiet defiance inspired the 381-day Montgomery bus boycott, mobilizing Montgomery's black community and resulting in a Supreme Court decision that Alabama laws requiring segregation on city buses were unconstitutional. This was the first major civil rights victory won through widespread public protests.

The success of the Montgomery bus boycott encouraged growing numbers of civil rights activists, black and white, to challenge laws that enforced segregation. Beginning in 1960, black high school and college students staged sit-in demonstrations at segregated lunch counters and restaurants in more than a hundred Southern cities. They took seats and refused to leave until they were served or arrested. As the sit-in movement spread, protestors tried to check out books at segregated public libraries, to occupy seats in white-only sections of movie theaters, to stage "sleep-ins" at segregated hotels and "wade-ins" at beaches reserved for whites.

Black and white demonstrators, guarded by police, conduct a wade-in at a segregated beach in St. Augustine, Florida, June 29, 1964.

Freedom riders gather outside their firebombed and burning bus on the outskirts of Anniston, Alabama, May 14, 1961.

Sit-ins led to Freedom Rides, as teams of black and white volunteers rode buses across the South, testing a Supreme Court ruling that ordered integration of all bus and train stations serving passengers traveling across state lines. Always the volunteers faced the looming threat of violence from white vigilantes determined to put an end to "race-mixing." "When we began the ride I think all of us were prepared for as much violence as could be thrown at us," said James Farmer, an organizer of the first Freedom Ride. "We were prepared for the possibility of death."

When Farmer's bus pulled into the Greyhound station in Anniston, Alabama, on May 14, 1961, it was met by an angry mob armed with clubs, bricks, iron pipes, and knives. The terrified passengers—nine freedom riders and five regular passengers—remained glued to their seats as the mob tried to pry open the bus door and began to slash the tires. The driver revved the engine, backed up, and raced away, escaping down Highway 78.

A few miles out of town, the bus began to list to one side as the slashed tires went flat. The driver pulled over to the side of the road, where the bus station mob, barreling down the highway in some fifty cars and pickup trucks, caught up with it. Surrounding the bus, they began to smash its windows with bricks and a heavy ax, and again tried to force open the door.

Someone threw a firebomb through a broken window, and the panic-stricken passengers, choking from the dense cloud of smoke, escaped through an emergency exit seconds before the bus burst into flames. They were saved from the fury of the mob when an undercover state police detective on board brandished his revolver, fired a shot into the air, and ordered the attackers to fall back. The mob dispersed as state troopers arrived with their weapons drawn. No one was arrested.

Farmer's brush with death was just one violent incident among many. White mobs attacked other groups of freedom riders at bus depots in Birmingham and Montgomery. While witnessing the Birmingham attack, a U.S. Justice Department attorney phoned his office. "Oh, there are fists, punching!" he cried. "A bunch of men led by a guy with a bleeding face are beating them. There are no cops. It's terrible! It's terrible! There's not a cop in sight. People are yelling, 'There those niggers are! Get 'em, get 'em!' It's awful!"

Freedom riders in Montgomery were beaten so severely that an FBI agent said he "couldn't see their faces through the blood." Reporters at the scene were also roughed up as enraged whites seized and smashed their cameras, clubbed the reporters to the floor, and chased them out of the bus depot.

In 1961, meanwhile, students meeting at a conference in Raleigh, North Carolina, agreed to form a new civil rights group. Inspired by the teachings of Mohandas Gandhi, they called themselves the Student Non-violent Coordinating Committee (SNCC, pronounced "snick" for short). They committed themselves to the spirit and practice of nonviolent resistance as a means of challenging segregation in all its forms. SNCC members played key roles in the sit-in movement and the Freedom Rides. Later they began to focus their efforts on what they regarded as the most crucial civil rights issue—securing the right of black citizens to vote. That seemed the most effective way to overthrow segregationist Jim Crow laws.

SNCC began voter registration campaigns in a few carefully chosen Mississippi and Alabama congressional districts. Early in 1963 two young SNCC field workers, Bernard and Colia Lafayette, announced that they would move to Selma, a town SNCC had given up on since recruiting black voters "was too hard" there. The city's mayor had served notice that "Selma does not intend to change its customs or way of life." In the past, as soon as SNCC workers had arrived they were arrested and run out of town.

The Lafayettes welcomed the challenge.

*Bernard Lafayette, at right,
stands with five other freedom
riders at the closed door of a
Greyhound bus in Birmingham,
Alabama, May 19, 1961. Drivers
refused to allow the racially mixed
group to board, and after two hours,
the bus was canceled. By the time
Lafayette began his field work in
Selma, he had been arrested
during Freedom Rides and sit-ins
at least ten times.*

Three

Selma's Students Lead the Way

Keeping a low profile, Bernard and Colia Lafayette walked the unpaved streets of Selma's black neighborhood, knocked on people's doors, and went from one sharecropper's house to the next out in the countryside, talking to folks about their rights as citizens. They held voter registration classes, showing people how to fill out the required forms, and encouraged them to go down to the courthouse and attempt to register. But they ran up against a wall of resistance. Few voting-age blacks were prepared to challenge the white employers and landowners who held the purse strings in Dallas County.

White folks owned and controlled nearly everything. They ran the schools and the local government. Blacks who tried to register faced threats, harassment, and loss of their jobs. "That boy ought to go home," one woman said of Lafayette. "He's gonna get the white people all stirred up, then he'll run back to Atlanta and we'll be picking up the pieces."

"It's not gonna come to a damn thing," a black merchant complained. "Somebody'll get their brains blown out."

The Lafayettes discovered that local authorities were listening in on their phone calls. One night, across the street from their apartment, Bernard was brutally assaulted and beaten by two white men. He spent the night in the hospital. When he was released in the morning he immediately went downtown, a walking advertisement for everyone to see, "eyes all swollen, face bruised, blood all over his shirt." A friend, J. L. Chestnut Jr., who would eventually become Selma's first black lawyer, urged Lafayette to go home, but he refused. "No way," he said. "This is the symbol we need." He continued to wear that blood-stained shirt for almost a month. His example was seen as "a turning point in terms of public sympathy in Selma," said Chestnut. "Even the blacks who were most apprehensive about him couldn't help but respect his commitment and courage."

Lafayette's reputation in the black community was raised another notch when he went to court to fight his arrest and jailing on a false charge of vagrancy. Sheriff Clark had accused him of begging in public. Since he was gainfully employed by SNCC, had no outstanding debts, and had plenty of cash in his wallet when arrested, the charge was groundless and, after a trial, had to be dropped.

Despite the improper arrest, the brutal beating, and constant surveillance, the Lafayettes continued to hold voter clinics. When additional SNCC workers arrived in Selma to join them, a local judge denounced them all as "Communist agitators." And when they held a protest at the courthouse, holding cardboard placards that read "Register To Vote" and "Register Now for Freedom Now," Sheriff Clark arrested them on the courthouse steps, cheered on by white bystanders shouting, "Get 'em, Big Jim! Get 'em!"

SNCC teamed up with the Dallas County Voters League, and together they planned a mass meeting at Selma's Tabernacle Baptist Church. At first, church officials opposed the

Demonstrators from the Student Nonviolent Coordinating Committee, holding placards urging black citizens to register as voters, are about to be arrested by Selma police, October 7, 1963.

Pastor H. C. McClain views the burned ruins of his High Hope Baptist Church, Dawson, Georgia, 1962. Black churches active in the civil rights movement were at risk of being burned or bombed.

meeting. They feared that their church, like many others active in the civil rights movement, would be bombed. But the pastor, the Reverend I. L. Anderson, insisted, and the meeting drew a crowd of several hundred people on the evening of May 14. 1963. Speaker after speaker urged the audience to demand their rights by marching to the courthouse and registering to vote. "Someday they will have to open up that ballot box," declared SNCC executive secretary James Forman as the crowd cried "Amen!"

Seated in the rear of the church was Sheriff Clark with a bunch of his armed deputies, recording the names of people who attended the meeting and taking notes on everything the speakers said. Other deputies stood by the church door, photographing people as they came in. Clark could not fail to see that the crowd that evening included a large number of teenagers, students at Hudson High, Selma's all-black high school. And SNCC staff members noted that the students were the most vocal and enthusiastic members of the audience. They had been inspired by press coverage of kids their age taking part in sit-ins, Freedom Rides, and protest marches, and they wanted to be part of the action.

Lafayette visited Hudson High, inviting student volunteers to join his cause. The principal threatened to have him arrested, but the students loved him. A sharp young guy with a thin mustache—he was just twenty-two—Lafayette spoke their language, and as a pioneering Freedom Rider, who had been arrested several times, he was a celebrity. "What Bernard was telling us was like opening a window to an entirely new world," recalled Charles Bonner, who was sixteen at the time. "We were totally prepared to take some action, against what my friend Cleo and I both saw as tremendous unfairness in the world. So that's what we did."

SNCC workers offered to train the students in tactics of nonviolent protest and resistance, teaching them how to organize marches and demonstrations and how to respond if they were arrested or attacked: "If you're beaten on, crouch and put your hands over the back of your head," demonstrators were advised. "Don't put up your arm to ward off a blow. If you fall, fall right down and look dead. . . . And listen! If you can't be nonviolent, let me know now."

The teenagers eagerly embraced the struggle that their parents and teachers had been avoiding. "The students, the sons and daughters of older black residents, started the political and social unrest in Selma," recalled Annie Lee Cooper. "SNCC had to use the students initially, otherwise the effort in Selma would have failed and there would have been no Selma campaign."

As the 1963–64 school year began, Hudson High students organized Selma's first lunch counter sit-in. Their arrests were followed by a protest march and more arrests. The sit-ins and marches continued almost daily, and by early October more than three hundred young people had been arrested.

Black students holding handwritten signs sing and chant as they stage a demonstration in front of the Dallas County Courthouse, February 5, 1965.

"When the police would stop the students," Mrs. Cooper said, "they would simply kneel down and pray. This angered the local police. The student numbers increased so much [that] the local jail could no longer hold them."

Johnny Manuel was a tenth grader that year. "It seemed like the young people were more fed up with the local situation than were the black adults," he recalled. "When things got started in Selma, the black adults wanted events to go slow. We, the students, wanted things to move faster. During the first semester of 1963, it did not take much for young black people to get involved."

Students joined the demonstrations in growing numbers, cutting classes so they could appear at that day's assigned meeting place. Algebra gave way to activism. Many of their teachers seemed sympathetic. The students, apparently, were doing what the teachers wished they could do themselves if their jobs were not at risk, and they looked the other way when students left school early or failed to show up.

This explosion of teenage activism alarmed some parents and took the white authorities by surprise. Sheriff Clark and his possemen responded with a show of force. They were always ready to start striking with their billy clubs and jabbing with electric cattle prods. They made mass arrests of students, sending them to the local jail, and when that was filled to capacity, to prison camps outside of town.

"We were held at Camp Thompson for seven days," recalled Bobby Thomas, a tenth grader at Hudson High. "We did not wash during this time. We were not permitted to wash.

"After seven days, we were taken back to Selma for a court hearing. We were charged with unlawful assembly. I remember the white judge coming out of his chambers and sniffing the air like an animal as he prepared to enter the courtroom." The judge turned around, returned to his chambers, came back to the courtroom with a can of air freshener, and sprayed the courtroom. "There were a couple of hundred of us crammed into the little courtroom who had not had any water on their bodies for seven days," recalled Thomas. "We were numb to the odor, but the smell was fresh in the judge's nostrils."

The authorities' tough tactics backfired. Rather than cowing the students into submission, the arrests stiffened their resolve, and they returned to the streets with renewed conviction. "We considered tak-

Student demonstrators on their way to jail.

ing a stand, being arrested, and going to jail to be an event that instilled the utmost pride," one student demonstrator explained.

Mass meetings were now being held weekly at Brown Chapel African Methodist Episcopal Church. Students came to the pulpit to tell of their experiences as demonstrators, while speakers from black churches around Dallas County urged adults in the audience to follow the students' example and get involved.

"After my son and daughter went to jail, I was determined to go also," said one mother. "I was moved

Sheriff Jim Clark uses his billy club to prod a demonstrator.

by what they were doing....My children had gone to jail for the cause of justice. I could not bear up under the thought of keeping my distance any longer. I was determined to do my part."

By now, voting-age adults were stepping forward and volunteering to join the cause of voter registration. By the summer of 1964, hundreds of black adults were standing in line outside the Dallas County Courthouse on registration days, waiting to be admitted so they could register. Perhaps twenty-five or thirty applicants would actually be examined by the registrars that day. Of those, possibly none would pass the written and oral exams. And yet the same people came back to stand in line again—an act of public protest for the world to see. The police photographed applicants standing in the courthouse line, and when local newspapers published the photos, some people lost their jobs.

At the height of the Selma campaign, on July 4, 1964, students trying to enter the segregated Wilby Theater and Thirsty Boy drive-in were attacked by whites and then arrested for trespassing. The next day, Sheriff Clark's deputies arrested demonstrators holding a rally at the courthouse.

"I'll never forget Clark emerging from the courthouse that afternoon," recalled John Lewis, a founding member of SNCC who in 1963 was elected chairman of the civil rights group. "I had seen [Clark's] anger many times, but this day he looked more furious than ever. You could see the rage just building up in him. He was a huge man—about six feet five, 230 pounds, maybe 240—and it seemed as if he was going to burst out of his clothes. . . . He was trembling, literally shaking with anger." As the demonstrators were marched five blocks to jail, singing freedom songs, they were repeatedly jolted by cattle prods.

After those arrests, a local circuit court judge, James A. Hare, issued an injunction forbidding public gatherings of more than three people. Mass meetings and marches were banned. Judge Hare was an outspoken segregationist who compared the voting rights demonstrators to terrorists. Selma had been "subjected to something fantastic and terroristic," he declared. "If these unsanitary, unbathed ruffians think we are going to lie down and give Selma over to them, they have another thought coming! I am not going to sit idly by while they destroy this city."

SNCC attorneys appealed Hare's ruling, but in the meantime the city warned that his court order would be strictly enforced. Black ministers would be arrested if they allowed mass meetings to be held at their churches. Marchers and demonstrators would be marched directly to jail.

Protest activity in Selma came to a standstill. In response, a group of men and women who had been active in the voting rights campaign began meeting secretly in homes and offices, discussing ways to overcome the court order and keep the protest movement alive. They agreed to appeal to the nation's best-known civil rights leader, the Reverend Martin Luther King Jr., head of the Southern Christian Leadership Conference (SCLC). Would Dr. King be willing to come to Selma, they asked, and help save their voter registration drive?

King had gained national prominence during the Montgomery bus boycott a decade earlier. His powerful "I have a dream" speech at the 1963 March on Washington, delivered from the steps of the Lincoln Memorial, won the admiration of people around the world. And his efforts had helped convince the U.S. Congress to pass the landmark Civil Rights Act of 1964, which outlawed discrimination in public accommodations such as restaurants, theaters, and hotels, in government, and in employment. That act, however, did not guarantee the right to vote, a battle that was now being fought in the streets of Selma.

King was about to leave for Oslo, where he would receive the 1964 Nobel Peace Prize from the king of Norway. On his return to America, he promised, he would come to Selma.

Four

"March, Dammit!"

Martin Luther King arrived at Selma's Brown Chapel on the evening of January 2, 1965, greeted by an exuberant crowd of seven hundred singing, clapping would-be voters. And King did not disappoint. In his rousing baritone voice, he called for massive street demonstrations if Alabama's blacks were not allowed to register as voters. "Today marks the beginning of a determined, organized, mobilized campaign to get the right to vote everywhere in Alabama," he told the crowd. "We must be ready to march. We must be ready to go to jail by the thousands. . . . Our cry to the state of Alabama is a simple one. Give us the ballot!"

King was followed at the pulpit by the Reverend Frederick Douglass Reese, president of Selma's black teachers' association. The time had come for the teachers to step forward, Reese declared. "If you will participate in a teachers march, sign this list," he called out to his fellow teachers in the audience. "We are going to march from Clark Elementary School to the courthouse on Friday, January 22. We are going as teachers and will request that the registrar's office be open and all of the teachers be allowed to register to vote." A black teachers' march would have a powerful impact, Reese predicted, because "neither the local whites nor the black population [expects] the teachers to do it."

This was Selma's first mass meeting in six months, since the court order banning marches and meetings. That ruling had been appealed to a federal court, where it was still pending, and city officials, worried about Selma's growing reputation as a segregationist trouble spot, had let it be known that the ban would no longer be enforced. Selma's mayor had ordered Sheriff Clark to avoid violent confrontations.

Speaking at Selma's Brown Chapel on January 2, 1965, Dr. Martin Luther King Jr. calls for massive voting rights demonstrations.

But the sheriff considered himself the highest law enforcement official in Dallas County. And black leaders, aware of Clark's segregationist views and explosive temper, expected him to display, for the world to see, the violence that assailed blacks when they tried to exercise their right to vote.

"Sheriff Jim Clark was the symbol of white resistance in the South," Reese recalled. "[We] knew how to get the sheriff to act in such a manner as to embarrass himself, the local civic authorities and city of Selma before the nation on television. Sheriff Clark never disappointed us and national news cameras in Selma never failed to record his actions and broadcast them to the world. Sheriff Clark always had his billy club and so did his deputies.... [He] would go absolutely crazy, as if he had lost all contact with reality...hitting and beating the black folk nearest him with his billy club. That was just what we wanted him to do so the world could see on the evening news what was happening in Selma."

The revived voting rights campaign began on January 18, when King led four hundred blacks in a march to the courthouse. Sheriff Clark ordered the marchers to line up in a roped-off back alley. There were no arrests that day, no one was admitted to the courthouse, and no blacks were registered.

Afterward, King and some of his SCLC aides went to the historic Hotel Albert, built by slave labor, to sign in as the hotel's first-ever black guests. As King stood at the registration desk while reporters, cameramen, and police looked on, a gaunt white man approached and said, "I'd like to see you a minute." Then, without warning, he began to punch and kick King until he was pulled away, wrestled across the hotel lobby's red carpet, and dragged to a patrol car. He was later identified as Jimmy George Robinson, a member of the seg-

Segregationist Jimmy George Robinson attacks Martin Luther King as the civil rights leader tries to register at Selma's Hotel Albert, January 18, 1965. Robinson, at center, is being wrestled away from the registration desk by bystanders, while the woman at left tries to avoid the altercation and King ducks.

regationist National States Rights Party. King wasn't injured, and he and his party were assigned hotel rooms in compliance with the recently passed Civil Rights Act.

The next day, demonstrators waiting to register at the courthouse refused to obey the sheriff's order to line up in the back alley where they had been confined the day before. Instead, they surged through the building's front door and defied Clark's order to leave. Sixty-seven demonstrators were arrested, among them Mrs. Amelia Boynton, a well-known local civil rights leader.

"Clark had a big club in his hand," she recalled. "Before I could gather my wits, he had left the steps and jumped behind me, grabbed me by my coat, propelled me around and started shoving me down the street. I was stunned. I saw cameramen and newspaper reporters around and...I said, 'I hope the newspapers see you acting this way.' He said, 'Dammit, I hope they do.'"

The teachers' turn to march came on January 22, when more than a hundred teachers followed Rev. Reese to the courthouse steps, were turned roughly away, and then marched back to Brown Chapel. Their march set an example for other middle-class blacks. "The undertakers got a group, and they marched," Reese recalled. "The beauticians got a group, they marched. Everybody marched after the teachers marched."

As the protest marches continued day after day, Sheriff Clark and his posse did not hesitate to get tough, shoving people and jabbing them with nightsticks when they stepped off the curb or out of line or did not move along fast enough. "The white law enforcement officers...always seem to be out in larger numbers than needed, in riot helmets, with an assortment of nightsticks, electric cattle prods and guns

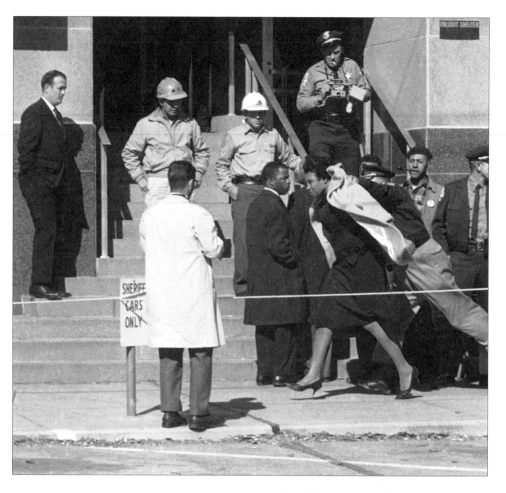

Sheriff Jim Clark grabs demonstrator Amelia Boynton by her coat collar and shoves her roughly down the street.

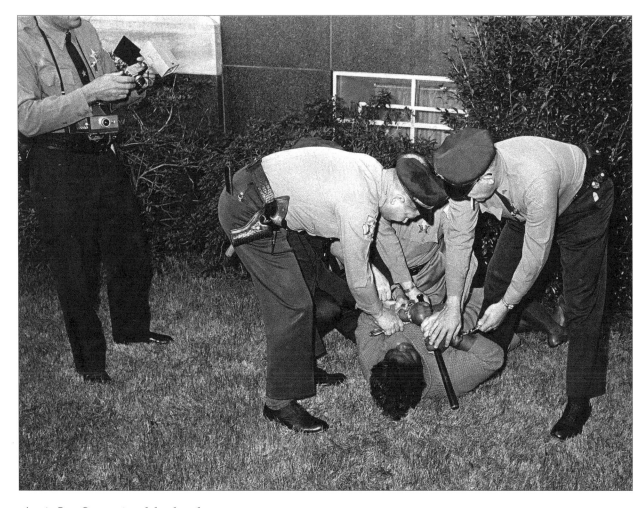

Annie Lee Cooper is subdued and handcuffed after slugging Sheriff Jim Clark and knocking him to the pavement.

hanging from their belts," reported John Herbers of the *New York Times*.

Not every demonstrator had the self-control to obey the discipline of nonviolent resistance championed by Dr. King. During one march, when Annie Lee Cooper, a large woman, stepped a few paces out of line, Sheriff Clark rushed up behind her, elbowing people aside, and shoved her so hard that she lost her balance. She swung around, hauled off, and slugged the sheriff in the face. He staggered to his knees and she punched him again.

Three deputies wrestled her to the ground, and as she kicked and struggled, Clark clubbed her with his nightstick. Mrs. Cooper, a motel clerk, was taken to jail in two pairs of handcuffs with a wound over her right eye. When reporters asked Clark if she was married, he replied, "She's a nigger woman and she hasn't got a Miss or Mrs. in front of her name."

"She put up quite a battle as the officers seized her and threw her to the ground," the *New York Times* reported. " 'I wish you would hit me you scum,' she snapped at the sheriff. He then brought his billy club down on her head with a whack that was heard throughout the crowd gathered in the street."

As it turned out, Mrs. Cooper had been trying to register for months. A year earlier, she had organized her fellow black employees at a white-owned nursing home to join a voter registration march.

When their employer came by and saw them standing in line at the courthouse, he fired them all. Mrs. Cooper eventually found another job as a clerk at a black-owned motel. Her battle with Sheriff Clark became part of the folklore of the voting rights campaign.

On February 1, King was himself arrested during a demonstration and led to jail with his associate the Reverend Ralph Abernathy. The two men refused to post the $200 bond required of nonresidents, and remained behind bars for five days before they were released.

Two years earlier, King's "Letter from a Birmingham Jail," published in newspapers around the world, had been greeted as an important defense of nonviolent resistance to unjust laws. Now, in his "Letter from a Selma Jail," he wrote: "When the King of Norway participated in awarding the Nobel Prize to me, he surely did not think that in less than 60 days I would be in jail. This is Selma, Alabama, where there are more Negroes in jail with me than there are on the voting rolls."

While King and Abernathy sat in jail, the city's students were out in the streets protesting their arrests. Every evening, television newscasts showed youngsters being led off to jail. Authorities sometimes held them for days without notifying their parents.

On February 10, Sheriff Clark and his possemen led 165 demonstrators, mostly teenagers and younger children, on a forced march into the countryside.

A police officer grabs Dr. King by the seat of his trousers and leads him to a paddy wagon during a demonstration in Birmingham, Alabama. King, along with other civil rights leaders, was arrested a number of times.

Teenagers and some younger children run to keep up with Sheriff Jim Clark, leading in a police car, during a two-and-a-half hour forced march out of Selma into the countryside.

The youngsters were standing silently outside the courthouse, displaying crayoned signs urging equal voting rights, when the sheriff ordered them to follow him down the street. "Move out!" he shouted, as his deputies herded them in single file down the middle of Alabama Avenue, heading toward the edge of town, while Clark and the deputies, using nightsticks and cattle prods, forced the students to move along faster, walking at first, then jogging, and then running. Some deputies followed in cars while others trotted beside the running youngsters, yelling, "You've been wanting to march, now let's go. Close up the ranks back there. Come on, close it up, close it up!"

About a mile and a half out of town, a deputy blocked the entrance to a bridge after the runners had passed over, and refused to let reporters and cameramen go any farther. The exhausted youngsters were forced to keep on running. When one girl stopped breathlessly, unable to go on, a deputy jabbed her with his club and shouted, "March, dammit. She's going to march!"

After running almost two and a half miles, the youngsters rebelled and fled into a private yard beside the road. Some stopped to vomit. Sheriff Clark tried to herd them back onto the road, but they refused to move. He finally gave up and drove back to Selma with his men.

When reporters reached the scene a half hour later, they found the young marchers in the yard singing freedom songs. One girl showed a lump on her head where, she said, a deputy had hit her. A nine-year-old boy stood in the yard with a tear-stained face and bare feet. He had made the march barefoot.

By the middle of February, nearly 3,400 demonstrators had been arrested, filling up the jails and several prison work camps in the area. Meanwhile, efforts by protest leaders to influence public opinion were beginning to pay off. A congressional delegation had traveled to Selma to investigate the mass arrests and determine if new legislation was needed to ensure voting rights. And President Lyndon B. Johnson had held a press conference to deliver a statement in support of voting rights. "All Americans should be indignant when one American is denied the right to vote," he told reporters. "The loss of that right undermines the freedom of every citizen."

By then, the demonstrations had spilled over into nearby towns. On February 18, the town of Marion became the scene of a bloody police riot. After a nighttime rally at a black church in the town square, four hundred people filed out the church doors and moved down a sidewalk lined by helmeted state troopers and deputy sheriffs. They were heading to the local jail to protest the arrest earlier that day of a civil rights worker. After walking half a block, they were ordered to stop. "This is an unlawful assembly," the police chief announced through a loudspeaker. "You are hereby ordered to disperse. Go home or go back to the church."

The column of demonstrators stretched all the way back to the church doors. Reporters standing across the street saw troopers struggling with someone at the front of the line. At that point, the streetlights were either turned off or perhaps shot out. Troopers waded into the crowd, swinging their nightsticks as people trying to get away screamed and stumbled over one another. At the same time, a crowd of white vigilantes attacked the reporters and smashed their cameras. No photographic record of the night survives.

Eighty-two-year-old Cager Lee had attended the church rally with his daughter, Viola, and grandson, twenty-six-year-old Jimmie Lee Jackson. The old man was bleeding from a head wound. Jackson and his mother hustled him into a nearby café that was already packed with people seeking refuge. Troopers stormed the café, smashed the lights, and began to club people. As Jackson tried to protect his mother, he was shoved up against a cigarette machine and shot twice in the stomach by a trooper later identified as James Fowler. He staggered out of the café, was clubbed on the head, and collapsed in the street, where he lay bleeding until he was taken to a hospital in Selma, thirty miles away.

Jackson was an army veteran who had tried five times to register to vote, without success. While he was in the hospital, he was served a warrant charging him with assault and battery with intent to murder a peace officer. But on February 26, eight days after the shooting, Jackson died.

"I knew it was only a matter of time until we got that news, but nonetheless it was very emotional," John Lewis recalled. "A lot of people had suffered during the previous two months. A lot of people had been beaten and hurt and jailed. But no one had died. Not until now."

"We was infuriated to the point that we wanted to carry Jimmy's body to [Governor] George Wallace and dump it on the steps of the capitol," said Albert Turner, a civil rights worker in Marion. At a mass meeting in Selma, King called for a "motorcade" of protesters—"carloads of people from all over the state to march on the capitol" in Montgomery. "We will be going there to tell Governor Wallace we aren't going to take it anymore."

Because many blacks could not afford to own cars, James Bevel, an SCLC leader and aide to King, suggested *walking* instead of driving the 54 miles to Montgomery, an idea that quickly caught fire. "The blood of Jackson will be on our hands if we don't march," Bevel declared. "Be prepared to walk to Montgomery. Be prepared to sleep on the highways."

So it was settled. The press was informed that a march from Selma to Montgomery would begin on Sunday, March 7, and that it would be led by Martin Luther King.

Five

Bloody Sunday

The casket bearing the body of Jimmie Lee Jackson is carried into Brown Chapel for funeral services. A handwritten banner draped over the church entrances reads: "Racism Killed Our Brother."

The once-sleepy city of Selma was now the storm center of the civil rights movement, and tensions were rising. Funerals for Jimmie Lee Jackson were held in both Selma and Marion. More than a thousand people walked three miles in the rain to the black cemetery in Marion. "Jimmie Lee Jackson is speaking to us from the casket," Dr. King told the mourners, "and he is saying to us that we must substitute courage for caution."

On Friday, March 5, two days before the planned march from Selma to Montgomery, King met with President Johnson at the White House. The president had been reluctant to push for voting rights legislation so soon after Congress passed the Civil Rights Act of 1964. But events of the past few weeks had changed Johnson's mind, and he assured King that a voting rights bill would soon be introduced in Congress.

In Montgomery, Governor Wallace told a press conference that Alabama would not permit the march to take place, because it would tie up traffic on U.S. 80, the main highway to the capital. "Such a march cannot and will not be tolerated,"

Wallace declared. He informed Selma's mayor, Joe Smitherman, that the marchers would be blocked peacefully, without violence. Smitherman wasn't so sure. The mayor and his public safety director, Wilson Baker, worried that Sheriff Clark and his good friend Colonel Al Lingo, commander of the state troopers, had plans of their own that could turn Sunday's march into a bloodbath.

On Saturday, March 6, the day before the march, tensions in Selma escalated when a group of seventy sympathetic whites from across the state held a rally of their own to support black voting rights. Standing on the courthouse steps, the Reverend Joseph Ellwanger declared, "We, as white citizens of Alabama, have come to Selma today to tell the nation that there are white people in Alabama who will speak out against the events that have recently occurred in this and other cities and towns. . . . We are horrified at the brutal way the police have attempted to break up peaceful assemblies and demonstrations."

Before Ellwanger could get very far into his speech, he was drowned out by a large crowd of hostile whites who began singing "Dixie." One of the whites was Jimmy George Robinson, who had assaulted King in the Albert Hotel. Ellwanger raised his voice, trying to be heard. His followers broke into a rousing chorus of "America the Beautiful." Across the street, a group of blacks responded with a thundering chorus of "We Shall Overcome." Before the musical confrontation could explode into a race riot, Selma's public safety director, Baker, persuaded the concerned whites to wrap up their rally and hurry back to the Reformed Presbyterian Church where they had first assembled. As they were leaving, Robinson ran up to a SNCC photographer and punched him in the face.

King had announced that he would come to Selma to lead the march. But the Justice Department warned of a possible plot on his life, one of several death threats he had received. When King's staff learned that state troopers would almost certainly block the march, they advised the civil rights leader to remain in Atlanta.

"We expected a confrontation," wrote John Lewis. "We knew Sheriff Clark had issued yet another

Alabama governor George C. Wallace. He vowed to prevent the March 7 voting rights march.

John Lewis and Hosea Williams led the march in the absence of Dr. King.

call for even more deputies. Mass arrests would probably be made. There may be injuries. Most likely we would be stopped at the edge of the city limits, arrested and maybe roughed up a little. We did not expect anything worse than that."

"None of us anticipated" or even "imagined that they would use the brutal methods to which they actually resorted," King explained later.

On Sunday afternoon, March 7, some six hundred people set out from Brown Chapel, walking two abreast in a long, orderly procession that stretched for several blocks. Leading the column in King's absence were SNCC chairman John Lewis and Hosea Williams, an SCLC leader and aide to King. Among the marchers were students and older folks, parents and children, carrying backpacks, bedrolls, and lunch bags. If the state police did not stop them, they expected the march to last at least four days, allowing plenty of time for press coverage. That morning they had been coached on how best to protect themselves from blows and from the effects of tear gas. Trailing the procession as it set out were four ambulances and ten volunteer doctors and nurses who had flown in from New York the night before.

"There was no singing, no shouting—just the sound of scuffling feet," Lewis remembered. "Dr. King used to say there is nothing more powerful than the rhythm of marching feet, and that was what this was, the marching feet of a determined people. That was the only sound you could hear."

They marched six blocks to Broad Street, turned left, and began to cross the Edmund Pettus Bridge,

Marchers cross the Alabama River on the Edmund Pettus Bridge at Selma.

which arches high above the Alabama River. Near the bridge entrance, a group of Sheriff Clark's armed pos-semen watched the procession pass but did not allow the ambulances to follow the marchers across the bridge.

A cold wind from the muddy river whipped at the marchers' coats. As they reached the crest of the bridge and started down the other side, they saw "a sea of blue-helmeted, blue-uniformed Alabama state

Alabama state troopers stand by their cars on U.S. Highway 80, waiting for marchers to come over the bridge.

troopers, line after line of them," stationed shoulder to shoulder across the four lanes of Highway 80. Gas masks hung from their belts. Behind the troopers were several dozen more of Sheriff Clark's possemen, fifteen of them on horseback. About a hundred white spectators looked on from the side of the road, laughing and hollering, waving a Confederate flag. And at a safe distance from the troopers, fifty silent blacks stood watching beside an old yellow school bus.

Reporters and cameramen had been confined to a car dealer's parking lot beside the highway. Sheriff Clark and Colonel Lingo sat in a car nearby.

The marchers approached down the slope of the bridge, walking slowly and silently. The troopers slipped gas masks over their faces and stood slapping their nightsticks against their hands. Speaking through a bullhorn, Major John Cloud ordered the marchers to stop and turn back: "This is an unlawful assembly. Your march is not conducive to the public safety. You are ordered to disperse and go back to your church or your homes."

"May we have a word with the major?" asked Hosea Williams.

"There is no word to be had," Cloud replied.

The two men exchanged a few more words. Then the major said, "You have two minutes to turn around and go back to your church."

The marchers did not move. Then they heard Cloud order, "Troopers, advance!"

The troopers rushed forward. Marchers at the front of the column "were swept to the ground screaming, arms and legs flying, and packs and bags went skittering across the grassy divider strip and onto the pavement on both sides," reported Roy Reed in the *New York Times*. "Those still on their feet retreated.... A cheer went up from the white spectators lining the south side of the highway."

The first casualty of the day was John Lewis, his skull fractured in the exact spot where he had been struck years earlier during a Freedom Ride. As panicked marchers scattered in all directions, Sheriff Clark's mounted possemen let loose with a rebel yell and charged, swinging bullwhips and rubber tubing wrapped in barbed wire.

SNCC chairman John Lewis, in the light coat, cringes on the ground as a trooper swings his club at Lewis's head. He was later hospitalized with a fractured skull.

"They spurred their horses and rode at a run into the retreating mass," reported Reed. "The Negroes cried out as they crowded together for protection, and the whites on the sidelines whooped and cheered."

"The horses were more humane than the troopers; they stepped over fallen victims," recalled Amelia Boynton. "As I stepped aside from a trooper's club, I felt a blow on my head.... Another blow by a trooper as I was gasping for breath knocked me to the ground and there I lay, unconscious."

A tear gas canister exploded, spewing a gray cloud over the scene. "The tear gas was strong and forced us to scatter," recalled Bobby Thomas, a Hudson High student at the time. "As we were scattering, I remember seeing Mrs. Margaret Moore, a schoolteacher, lying on the ground at the foot of the bridge. I do not know if Mrs. Moore was hit, trampled, or just passed out. It was chaotic."

Clouds of tear gas obscure the scene as troopers rout the marchers and drive them back over the bridge. A raised club can be seen on the left.

Mounted possemen look on as a state trooper approaches an unconscious woman.

Forty tear gas canisters were fired that day. The marchers, blinded and choking, stumbled back onto the bridge and began a hasty retreat as troopers and possemen went after them on foot and on horseback.

"A burst of tear gas began," recalled Sheyann Webb, then eight years old. "I could see the troopers and policemen swinging their billy clubs. People began to run, and dogs and horses began to trample them.

You could hear people screaming and hollering. And I began to run....All I wanted to do was make my way back home. As I got almost down to the bottom of the bridge, Hosea Williams picked me up. I told him to put me down, 'cause he wasn't running fast enough."

Waiting at the Selma side of the bridge were the possemen who had watched the marchers pass earlier. They charged into the fleeing crowd on foot while possemen on horseback chased the marchers all the way back to the black section of town and Brown Chapel.

A makeshift clinic had been set up in the small parsonage beside the church. Doctors and nurses administered first aid for cuts and bruises and the effects of tear gas as marchers lay moaning and weeping on couches, chairs, and the floor. At least ninety marchers were wounded. Those with fractured ribs and wrists or serious head wounds were sent to Good Samaritan Hospital several blocks away. In the street outside the church, hundreds of angry blacks milled about as SCLC and SNCC staff members circulated among them, urging calm and nonviolence.

An injured marcher is carried from the scene.

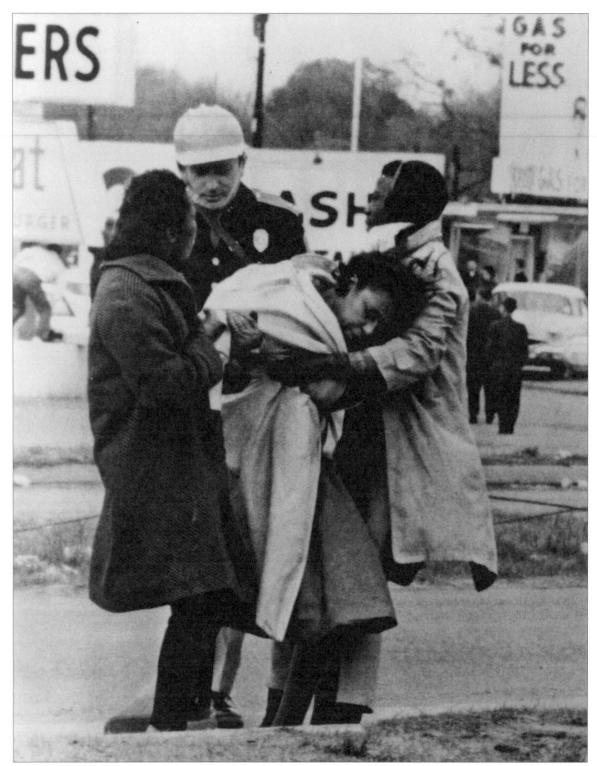

Inside the church, SCLC staffers were on the phone with King, telling him what had happened that day—soon to be known as "Bloody Sunday"—and discussing their next move. They decided that a call should go out to civil rights supporters all over the country, asking them to join King in a second attempt to march to Montgomery in two days, on Tuesday, March 9.

"In the vicious maltreatment of defenseless citizens of Selma, where old women and young children were gassed and clubbed at random, we have witnessed an eruption of the disease of racism which seeks to destroy all America," King declared. "No American is without responsibility."

Six

Turnaround Tuesday

As the bloodied marchers of Selma were being carried off to the hospital, the nation's three major television networks interrupted their scheduled programs and stunned viewers with graphic footage of the day's violence. Reporters had been kept at a distance from the action, but their telephoto lenses had captured almost the entire attack—"the flailing clubs, the stampeding horses, the jeering crowd and the stricken, fleeing blacks."

It was all on film. Unarmed men, women, and children on a highway were attacked by uniformed men wearing gas masks and riding horses. "It looked like war," Selma mayor Smitherman recalled. "[Television coverage] went all over the country. And the people, the wrath of the nation came down on us."

In the halls of Congress, lawmakers rose one after another to denounce Sunday's attack and demand new voting rights legislation. New York Senator Jacob Javits called the assault on the marchers "an exercise in terror."

On Monday, civil rights attorneys asked federal judge Frank M. Johnson Jr. to issue an injunction, forbidding the state of Alabama to interfere with Tuesday's planned march. But Judge Johnson was not a man to be hurried. He scheduled a hearing on the matter for Thursday of that week and ordered that no march could take place before then.

King and his staff now faced a tough decision. Should they cancel Tuesday's march? Or should they ignore Judge Johnson's order and go ahead with the march as planned?

Dr. King (second from left) and his associates listen silently as a federal marshal reads a court order prohibiting a Selma-to-Montgomery march until a hearing can be held.

Hundreds of people from all over the country had flocked to Selma, eager to take part in the second march. Some, unable to book space on scheduled flights, had chartered planes. King felt that it would be wrong to disappoint them, but still he hesitated. He did not want to defy a federal judge, something he had never done before. He needed the support of the federal courts. And he knew that Judge Johnson was sympathetic to the civil rights movement. Johnson was a member of a three-judge panel that had ruled bus segregation laws unconstitutional. Governor Wallace had called the judge "a low-down, carpet-baggin', scalawaggin', race-mixin' liar," a solid recommendation in some folks' view.

That night, when King addressed the overflow crowd crammed into Brown Chapel, he seemed "unusually subdued," according to some observers. He assured his listeners that the march to Montgomery would be attempted again the next day, but at the same time, he "gave the distinct impression that he was involved in some protracted struggle with his conscience."

Early Tuesday morning, King met privately with an official from the Justice Department who proposed a token march as a compromise. If the marchers crossed the Pettus Bridge to where the troopers were waiting, then turned around and walked back into Selma, there would be no violence and the demonstrators would have made their point. King listened but made no promises. Even if he tried to turn the procession around at the far end of the bridge, he was not certain that the marchers would follow his lead.

At Brown Chapel on Tuesday morning, several speakers defended the protesters' right to march despite Judge Johnson's order. When King arrived early that afternoon he announced, "We march." The crowd erupted into cheers. King turned to an aide and said softly, "But we might not march very far."

Within minutes, some 1,500 marchers had lined up and started to move out. "There were young blondes in polo coats and hipsters with beards, and the wives of Senators; there were white faces and black faces, ministers' collars and turtleneck sweaters. They differed in age and religion, but they shared a unity of purpose," reported Gay Talese of the *New York Times*.

Some marchers hoisted signs in the air: "Police intimidation enslaves us all"; "Silence is no longer golden." Some sang. Three marchers wearing shiny steel helmets identified themselves as construction workers. "I ain't gonna get bopped this time," one man said.

Following the same route they had taken on Sunday, the marchers reached the entrance to the Pettus Bridge, then continued across the bridge to U.S. Highway 80, where state troopers were waiting. Once

again, Major Cloud spoke through his bullhorn: "You are ordered to stop and stand where you are. This march will not continue."

King brought the marchers to a halt. "We have a right to march," he replied. "There is also a right to march to Montgomery."

Major Cloud repeated his order. King asked if the marchers could pray. "You can have your prayer," the major said.

King asked everyone to kneel, and 1,500 marchers in a line stretching back almost a mile sank to their knees. Prayers were offered by two ministers and a rabbi. As the crowd rose to its feet, Cloud abruptly turned and ordered the troopers to step aside, clearing the road and inviting King to defy the federal court order. Instead King wheeled around, and to almost everyone's surprise, each rank in the column wheeled in turn as he began to lead the marchers back to Selma.

"All of a sudden I realized that the people in front were turning around and coming back," one marcher recalled, "and I was aghast. What is going on? Are we not going through with this confrontation? What's happening?"

Some of the marchers were angry that King had agreed to a token march without their knowledge. They felt betrayed, and it would take a while for tempers to cool. And yet most of those in the march seemed relieved that they would not find themselves threatened—some for a second time—by the whips and clubs of "Alabama's storm troopers." There had been no violence. "That's a kind of victory in itself," said one marcher.

As they headed back to Brown Chapel they broke into a joyful freedom song, "We Love Everybody," adding new verses in the nonviolent tradition as they moved along: "We love Governor Wallace in our heart," and "We love the state troopers in our heart." That day became known as "Turnaround Tuesday."

Alabama state troopers watch and wait as 1,500 marchers cross the Edmund Pettus Bridge in a second attempt to march to Montgomery, March 9, 1965.

In a line stretching back nearly a mile, marchers kneel on the highway to pray.

"We knew we would not get to Montgomery," King told reporters. "We knew we would not get past the troopers, and we agreed that we would not break through the lines." He had not wanted to violate the court order, he said, but he felt that the marchers had to confront the state troopers to demonstrate their resolve. "I did it to give them an outlet," he explained. "If I had not done it, the pent up emotions, the inner tensions…would have exploded into retaliatory violence." And he pledged that they would march to Montgomery no matter how long it took.

Tuesday's march ended peacefully. But as darkness fell, three white Unitarian ministers who had come to Selma to take part in the march were assaulted by a gang of whites as they left a restaurant. The Reverend James J. Reeb from Boston was clubbed in the head. He fell into a coma and died two days later from a massive skull fracture. He was thirty-eight years old and the father of four. His death provoked a national outcry and massive sympathy marches in cities across the North.

From the White House, President Johnson announced that he was determined to press for a powerful new voting rights law. On the night of Monday, March 15, as seventy million Americans watched on television, the president made his case before a joint session of Congress.

"It is wrong—deadly wrong," he said, "to deny any of your fellow Americans the right to vote in this country.…[The black American's] actions and protests, his courage to risk safety, and even to risk his life, have awakened the conscience of this nation."

Selma, the president continued, marked a turning point in American race relations and American history. What happened there was "part of a far larger movement…the effort of American Negroes to secure for themselves the full blessings of American life." Johnson ended his speech by invoking the civil rights movement's favorite freedom song, its anthem and its most compelling theme: "Their cause must be our cause too. Because it is not just Negroes, but really all of us who must overcome the crippling legacy of bigotry and injustice. And, we *shall* overcome."

Martin Luther King watched the president's speech in Selma with colleagues and friends. "We were all sitting around together," the Reverend C. T. Vivian recalled, "and when LBJ said, 'We shall overcome,' we

Dr. King addresses the crowd following their aborted march on "Turnaround Tuesday."

all cheered. And I looked over…and Martin was very quietly sitting in the chair, and a tear ran down his cheek." None of them had ever seen King cry before. "It was a victory like no other. It was an affirmation of the movement," Vivian concluded.

Two days later, Judge Frank Johnson handed down his decision on the proposed Selma-to-Montgomery march. He ruled that the demonstrators had a legal and constitutional right to carry out that march, and that state and local officials were forbidden to interfere.

Seven

A Good Day to Be Alive

On Sunday morning, March 21, marchers assembled at Brown Chapel for the third time in two weeks. By now, the original group of five hundred had expanded to an exuberant, noisy throng of 3,200 blacks and whites from all over the country, including many who had never marched before and others who had been demonstrating against racial injustice for years. They laughed and cheered as Rev. Abernathy told them, "When we get to Montgomery, we are going to Governor Wallace's door and say, 'George, it's all over now. We've got the ballot.' "

The marchers were all but surrounded by scores of reporters and cameramen, who would follow every step of the way on their five-day trek along Highway 80. Hundreds of U.S. Army and National Guard troops patrolled Selma that day and lined the highway leading out of town. The troops had been dispatched by President Johnson after Governor Wallace had denounced the marchers as "Communist-trained agitators" and insisted that Alabama could not afford to pay state troopers to protect them.

After a flurry of last-minute preparations and speeches, marshals quickly arranged the marchers in a column, six abreast, and the march finally got under way at 12:47 p.m. The day was sunny and cool

More than 3,000 voting rights supporters assemble at Brown Chapel, beginning a third attempt to march to the state capitol in Montgomery, March 21, 1965.

as the mile-long procession headed for the Pettus Bridge. The marchers sang as they moved along, ignoring hecklers along the route who shouted racist slurs and held up signs with handwritten messages such as "Yankee trash go home."

Leading the procession along with Dr. King and other civil rights leaders were an Episcopal bishop, a Jewish rabbi, a United Nations diplomat, and four Catholic nuns wearing long black habits. "This is a great day to be alive," exclaimed Sister Mary Leoline from Kansas City. The ranks of marchers included many teenagers, small children with their parents, and a couple from California pushing a baby carriage.

James Letherer, a one-legged amputee from Saginaw, Michigan, would walk the entire distance with the aid of crutches and the helping hands of fellow marchers. Cager Lee, the eighty-two-year-old grandfather of Jimmie Lee Jackson, killed by a state trooper two weeks earlier, could walk only a few miles each day. But he always returned the next day, saying, "Just got to tramp some more." Seventeen-year-old Joe Boone from Selma, arrested seventeen times during the voting rights campaign, said that his parents never thought this day would come. "But it's here, and I want to do my part."

Catholic nuns join their fellow marchers for a rest stop on the first day of the march.

Amputee James Letherer from Saginaw, Michigan, marched the entire 54-mile distance on crutches.

Marching along U.S. Highway 80, named in honor of the president of the Southern Confederacy.

"The teenagers were a great inspiration," Amelia Boynton recalled. "I was much impressed with a fifteen-year-old Selma boy, [Leroy] Moton. His face beamed with pride as he carried the American flag.... Every now and then he would burst into song and we would join him."

Major Cloud and Sheriff Clark rode in a patrol car at the head of the march part of the way. Reporters asked Clark if he had any feelings about the event. "No," he replied. "I'm glad to get rid of the ones that are leaving [Selma], but I wish they'd come back and get the rest of them."

The marchers reached their first night's campsite at 5:30 p.m., having covered a little more than seven miles. Waiting for them were four carnival-sized rented tents, pitched in a black farmer's field. Just down the road, Highway 80 narrowed from four lanes to two. A federal court order limited the number of marchers to three hundred along the two-lane stretch across Lowndes County, where four out of five residents were black and not one was registered to vote. At that point, 2,900 of the 3,200 marchers were bused back to Selma, where many would stay as guests of black families until rejoining the marchers near Montgomery. The core group of three hundred would spend four nights at campsites along the way.

Each day a team of volunteers in Selma shuttled food and supplies to the campsites. "I was responsible for preparing three meals a day for the marchers," recalled Bernice Morton. Her day began at 2:30 a.m. when she drove to Green Street Baptist Church where the meals were prepared. "The food was shipped via Hertz rental trucks in thirty-gallon steel cans and had to be at the campsite by 6:30 a.m. After sending breakfast out, I returned home and started getting my children ready for school. After they were off, I returned to the church and started preparing lunch with my team....

"The Ku Klux Klan and the White Citizens Council would block the route and prevent the trucks with the food from getting through to the campsite. A couple of times, the drivers came back to the church saying that they were cut off and there was no alternate route to the site."

The road to Montgomery led the marchers through cotton fields and scraggly pine thickets, across twisting rivers and creeks, and into dark, gloomy swamps where dead trees draped with gray Spanish moss hugged the roadside. Along the way, sharecropping families came down to the road to wave and offer food. At one small town, a group of old folks and barefoot children rushed over to embrace Dr. King. They had been waiting four hours. "Will you march with us?" King asked an elderly man with a cane. "I'll walk one step, anyway," the man replied, "because I know for every step I'll take, you'll take two."

"To me, there was never a march like this one before, and there hasn't been one since," John Lewis wrote. "The incredible sense of community—of *communing*—was overwhelming. We felt bonded with one another, with the people we passed, with the entire nation."

"The racists see before them something more than voting rights," observed Elizabeth Hardwick, a New York writer who joined the march. "They sense the elation, the unexpected release. Few of us have shared any life as close as those 'on location' in the Civil Rights Movement. Shared beds and sofas, hands caressing the shoulders of little children, smiles and a spreading comradeship, absorption: this is…a great experience." In Hardwick's eyes, "The police, protected by their helmets, are frightened and confused by these seizures of happiness."

Monday night's camp was on the property of Mrs. Rosie Steele, a seventy-eight-year-old widow. "At first I didn't think [the march] amounted to much," she told a reporter. "I guess I've lived too long and just didn't think things would change—until I heard the president speak the other night. I knew [then that] he was my president too.…When they come to me and asked me if they could use my land I felt I couldn't afford to turn them down. If the president can take a stand, I guess I can too.…I don't know, I almost feel like I might live long enough to vote myself."

On Tuesday the marchers, drenched by torrential downpours, trudged along in their plastic ponchos, singing in the rain. They camped that night in a muddy field, sleeping on air mattresses resting on a thick bed of hay, which the tent crew had sprinkled on the oozing mud under the tents.

On Wednesday morning, the band of three hundred reached the point where the highway widened back to four lanes, ending the court's limitation on the number of marchers. As the day passed, cars and buses kept stopping alongside the moving procession, discharging new marchers who had flocked to

Along the way, sharecropping families came down to the highway to greet the marchers and wave them on.

Montgomery to walk the last few miles to the capitol. By late afternoon, the marchers' ranks were packed with thousands of newcomers carrying banners and placards telling where they were from and why they had come.

Mrs. Ann Cheatham, a housewife from England, had flown across the Atlantic just to take part in the last phase of the march. "I came to show that the English are in sympathy," she said. "People say it's not my business, but I would deny that. It's everybody's business."

At the final campsite just outside Montgomery, the continuously growing mass of demonstrators were treated to a four-and-a-half-hour outdoor stage show organized by Harry Belafonte and performed by some of the most popular entertainers of the day, among them Joan Baez, Pete Seeger, Tony Bennett, and Nina Simone. The crowd clapped along with the singers, laughed at the comedians, and sang folk songs and songs of the movement. Peter, Paul, and Mary set the tone by singing "The Times They Are A-changin'."

By Thursday morning, the fifth and last day of the march, more than twenty-five thousand people were striding six abreast through a misty drizzle toward the state capitol as army helicopters clattered overhead and troops stationed on rooftops watched for snipers and other signs of trouble. Leading the way, wearing special bright orange jackets, were the three hundred mostly young marchers who had walked the entire distance from Selma. "Make way for the originals!" the marshals shouted, forming a cordon to hold back the other marchers and the press. Behind the three hundred came Martin Luther King and all the other notables.

"The marchers pushed down the street joyfully, singing 'We Shall Overcome' at the top of their lungs," Roy Reed of the *New York Times* reported. "Rain and all, the entry into Montgomery had a grandeur that was almost biblical."

"When the marchers arrived from Selma, we were there to greet them," said Gladis Williams, a Montgomery high school student and member of the welcoming committee. "Thousands were there. Joy! That's what you felt.... They had come fifty miles but when you're marching and singing, it doesn't faze you how far it is."

An estimated 25,000 demonstrators fill the street in front of the Alabama state capitol, March 25, 1965.

The silver-and-white capitol building was flying the Alabama state flag and the stars and bars of the Confederate banner. The only American flags on display were those carried by the marchers. Governor Wallace refused to receive a delegation from the marchers. But he was spotted several times peeking out at the crowd from behind the drawn venetian blinds on his office windows.

Speaking from the steps of the capitol, prominent civil rights leaders and ordinary citizens recalled the turbulent events at Selma that had turned the voting rights campaign into a mass protest against racial injustice. "We are on the move now," Martin Luther King promised in the last speech of the day. "Yes, we are on the move and no wave of racism can stop us.... We must come to see that the end we seek is a society at peace with itself, a society that can live with its conscience." But he also warned that "difficult days" still lay ahead, that "We are still in for a season of suffering."

The rally ended as twenty-five thousand voices joined in singing "We Shall Overcome," changing the words to express the triumphant spirit of the day: "We *have* overcome today."

As the great crowd dispersed, marchers and visitors scrambled to find taxis, buses, cars, trains, and planes so they could get out of town before nightfall. They had been warned to leave Montgomery as quickly as they could, so as not to provide targets for angry segregationists.

Volunteers had arranged to drive some of the demonstrators back to Selma. After dropping off one group of marchers at Brown Chapel that evening, Viola Liuzzo, a thirty-nine-year-old mother of five from Detroit, headed back toward Montgomery to pick up another group. She was accompanied by Leroy Moton, a skinny, bespectacled black teenager who had carried an American flag during the march.

On a lonely stretch of Highway 80, they were overtaken by a carload of Ku Klux Klansmen who pulled alongside them. As Mrs. Liuzzo turned to look at them, one Klansman drew his pistol, put his arm out the car window, and shot Liuzzo twice in the face, killing her instantly and spewing blood over Moton.

Waving flags and singing freedom songs, the triumphant marchers stand before the capitol building. Dr. and Mrs. King are at front and center.

Liuzzo's car swerved off the highway and crashed into a ditch. When the Klansmen came over to inspect the wreckage, Moton pretended to be dead. After they left, the frightened youngster was able to flag down a passing car on the highway. The murderers were arrested within hours because one of the Klansmen was actually an undercover FBI informant who, as he later testified, had tried to persuade the others to give up the chase.

The murder of Viola Liuzzo was a reminder that a historic march and a joyful rally did not overcome the threat of racist violence, and that the "season of suffering" predicted by Dr. King still lay ahead.

The bullet-shattered window and blood-stained door of the car driven by Viola Liuzzo when she was shot and killed by a Ku Klux Klansman.

Eight

Because They Marched

As the swelling throng marched singing into Montgomery, the Voting Rights Act was beginning its own contested journey through the political thickets of Congress. Lawmakers from Southern states argued that the federal government should not have the power to interfere with a state's constitutional right to impose its own voting requirements. But most congressmen felt that the time had come to correct an injustice.

"Recent events in Alabama, involving murder, savage brutality, and violence by local police, state troopers, and posses have so aroused the nation as to make action by the Congress necessary and speedy," New York congressman Emanuel Celler declared.

After more than four months of debate, both the House of Representatives and the Senate voted by overwhelming margins to approve the Voting Rights Act of 1965. Support for the legislation was so widespread that several Southern lawmakers cast their first vote ever for a civil rights bill. "You know, you can't stop this bill," said Senator Harry Byrd of Virginia. "We can't deny the Negroes a basic constitutional right to vote."

President Johnson signed the Voting Rights Act on August 6 in the ornate President's Room of the Capitol as Martin Luther King, Rosa Parks, and other civil rights leaders looked on. In the same room

President Lyndon B. Johnson gives Dr. Martin Luther King one of the pens used to sign the landmark Voting Rights Act of 1965.

on the same date in 1861, one hundred and four years earlier, President Abraham Lincoln had signed a bill freeing slaves impressed into the service of the Confederate army.

"Today is a triumph for freedom as huge as any victory that has ever been won on any battlefield," Johnson said. "This act flows from a clear and simple wrong. Its only purpose is to right that wrong. Millions of Americans are denied the right to vote because of their color. This law will insure them the right to vote."

On August 20, two weeks after the president signed the act, Cager Lee, whose father had been sold in a slave market, registered to vote.

The Voting Rights Act has been called the crowning achievement of the civil rights movement. The act, in effect, abolished poll taxes, literacy tests, and other barriers to equal opportunity at the ballot box. And it sent federal examiners to counties in the South and elsewhere "where past experience" had shown that federal action was needed to register all eligible voters.

With the act's passage, African Americans finally gained the full political power so long denied them. The federally guaranteed right to vote gave them the opportunity to elect officials who would protect all the other basic rights guaranteed by federal law and the Constitution. Congress later expanded the law to include Hispanic, Asian, Native American, and other minority citizens, and in so doing, transformed America's political landscape.

Martin Luther King did not live to witness that transformation. On the evening of April 4, 1968, as he stood on a motel balcony in Memphis, Tennessee, waiting to go to dinner, he was killed by a single bullet from a high-powered hunting rifle. King was thirty-nine years old. It has never been determined whether his assassin, a white petty criminal named James Earl Ray, acted alone, as he claimed, or as part of a conspiracy.

The impact of the Voting Rights Act, meanwhile, was already being felt. By the summer following passage of the law, nine thousand blacks in Dallas County had been registered to vote. That year, 1966, black voters helped turn Dallas County Sheriff Jim Clark out of office, ending his political career.

In 2000, James Perkins Jr. was elected as Selma's first African-American mayor. By 2009, thousands of black, Hispanic, and Asian elected officials throughout the country were serving at all levels of government, from county sheriff to state governor to members of Congress to, finally, president of the United States.

When Barack Obama was campaigning for the presidency in 2007, he spoke at a ceremony in Selma commemorating the forty-second anniversary of the march to Montgomery. "It is because they marched," Obama told his audience, "that I stand here before you today."

Epilogue

In 2013 the Supreme Court struck down a key provision of the Voting Rights Act of 1965. The controversial 5–4 decision in *Shelby County v. Holder* released nine states, mostly in the South, from the requirement that they must seek advance federal approval before making any change in their election laws.

"Our country has changed," Chief Justice John G. Roberts Jr. wrote for the majority, arguing that the law's original requirements were no longer justified. He added that Congress remained free to impose federal oversight on states where voting rights were at risk, but must do so on the basis of current conditions.

In her dissenting opinion, Justice Ruth Bader Ginsberg drew sharply different lessons from the history of the civil rights movement. While some barriers to voting have been abolished, she said, discrimination at the ballot box continues in different forms and is growing. She cited the words of Martin Luther King, declaring that his legacy and the nation's commitment to justice had been "disserved by today's decision." Congress, she argued, was the right body to decide whether the law was still needed.

Immediately after the decision, some states and counties in the South announced that they would take advantage of the ruling to make legal changes in voting requirements—such as strict voter ID laws—that, critics say, would make it harder for minority voters, older people, students, legal immigrants, and the poor of all races to register and vote.

President Obama announced that he was "deeply disappointed" by the Supreme Court ruling. And longtime congressman John Lewis, a veteran civil rights activist and moving spirit of the 1965 march from Selma to Montgomery, denounced the ruling as a major blow to minorities in the United States. "It is awful, it's a sad day," he said. "I never thought that I would see the day when the U.S. Supreme Court would put a dagger in the heart of the Voting Rights Act of 1965."

And so the times are changing still. The right to vote continues to be challenged, and the meaning of American democracy remains a topic of debate and struggle, as it has since the nation's founding through the Civil War to Selma, and beyond.

Ballot box poster.

TIME LINE

1954	The U.S. Supreme Court outlaws segregation in the nation's public schools.
1955	Rosa Parks refuses to give up her seat on a city bus, beginning the year-long Montgomery bus boycott.
1960	The sit-in movement begins when four black students take seats at a Woolworth's lunch counter in Greensboro, North Carolina.
1961	The first freedom riders, seven black and six white volunteers, leave Washington, D.C., on buses bound for Alabama and Mississippi.
1962–63	SNCC field workers begin a voter registration project in Selma, Alabama.
1963	Martin Luther King Jr. delivers his "I have a dream" speech at the March on Washington for Jobs and Freedom, August 28.
1964	Dr. King is awarded the Nobel Peace Prize, October 14.
1965	
January 18	The voting rights campaign begins in Selma with a march led by Dr. King.

February 18   Jimmie Lee Jackson is shot by an Alabama state trooper during a voting rights demonstration in Marion, Alabama. His death six days later inspires plans to march from Selma to Montgomery.

March 7   On a day remembered as "Bloody Sunday," six hundred voting rights marchers are attacked by state troopers and sheriff's deputies as they cross Selma's Edmund Pettus Bridge.

March 9   In a second attempt to march to Montgomery, 1,200 marchers confront waiting state troopers, kneel on the highway to pray, then return to Selma on "Turnaround Tuesday."

March 15   President Lyndon B. Johnson, in a nationally televised speech to Congress, calls for voting rights legislation.

March 21–25   Voting rights demonstrators complete the 54-mile Alabama Freedom March and hold a rally at the state capitol attended by twenty-five thousand people.

August 6   President Johnson signs the Voting Rights Act of 1965.

1967   Thurgood Marshall is sworn in as the first African American Supreme Court justice.

1968   Martin Luther King is assassinated in Memphis, Tennessee, April 4.

SOURCE NOTES

One: The Day the Teachers Marched

"How can you...to register?" Vaughn, p. 44.

"Students who were...the courthouse." Ibid., p. 46.

"You pay...Keep moving." Ibid., p. 47.

"I can't...to town!" Fager, p. 38.

"illegal attempt...board is open." John Herbers, "Negro Teachers Protest in Selma," *New York Times*, January 23, 1965.

"Dr. Reese...our courthouse." Vaughn, p. 47.

"a stern-faced man...220 pounds." Herbers, "Negro Teachers Protest," *New York Times*, January 23, 1965.

"You can't make...clear the steps.," Ibid.

"The deputies...get arrested." Vaughn, pp. 47–48.

"I knew...hero's welcome." Vaughn, pp. 48–49

Two: White Folks' Business

"white folks' business." Williams, p. 252.

"The written test...was wrong." Vaughn, p. 65.

"Black people...their jobs." Ibid, p. 73

"That fire...quenched." Ibid., p. 73.

"They boycotted...my heart." Ibid., p. 66.

"When I was...mystifying." Levine, p. 14.

"Drinking fountains...at the front." Vaughn, p. 88.

"You had to...'a good Negro.' " Adam Liptak, "Voting Rights Act Is Challenged as Cure the South Has Outgrown," *New York Times*, February 18, 2013.

"We drew up...put on them." Vaughn, pp. 65–66.

"When we began...of death." Williams, p. 148.

"Oh, there are fists...It's awful!" Branch, *Parting the Waters*, p. 447.

"couldn't see...the blood." Weisbrot, p. 57.

"was too hard." May, p. 5.

"Selma does not...of life." Ibid., p. 7.

Three: Selma's Students Lead the Way

"That boy...blown out." May, p. 13.

"eyes all swollen...and courage." Ibid., p. 21.

"Communist agitators." Weisbrot, p. 128.

"Register...Freedom Now." Branch, *Pillar of Fire*, p. 555.

"Get 'em...get 'em!" Weisbrot, p. 129.

"Someday...ballot box." Branch, *Pillar of Fire*, p. 84.

"What Bernard...we did." May, p. 16.

"If you're beaten...know now." Adler, "Letter from Selma."

"The students...Selma campaign." Vaughn, p. 93.

"When the police...hold them." Ibid., p. 89.

"It seemed...get involved." Ibid., p. 143.

"We were held...judge's nostrils." Ibid., p. 139.

"We considered...utmost pride." Ibid., p. 131.

"After my son...do my part." Ibid., p. 101.

"I'll never forget...shaking with anger." Lewis, p. 312.

"subjected to something...destroy this city." May, p. 39.

Four: "March, Dammit!"

"Today marks...the ballot!" Branch, *Pillar of Fire*, p. 555.

"If you will...to do it." Vaughn, p. 44.

"Sheriff Jim Clark...in Selma." Ibid., p. 41.

"I'd like to see you a minute." Branch, *Pillar of Fire*, p. 561.

"Clark had...hope they do." Williams, p. 259.

"The undertakers...teachers marched." Ibid., p. 260.

"The white law...their belts." John Herbers, "Negro Goals in Selma," *New York Times*, February 6, 1965.

"She's a...in the street." John Herbers, "Woman Punches Alabama Sheriff," *New York Times*, January 26, 1965.

"When the King...voting rolls." Garrow, *Protest at Selma*, p. 52.

"Move out!" Branch, *Pillar of Fire*, p. 556.

"You've been...going to march!" Roy Reed, "165 Selma Negro Youths Taken on Forced March," *New York Times*, February 11, 1965.

"All Americans...every citizen." Garrow, *Protest at Selma*, p. 51.

"This is...the church." John Herbers, "Negroes Beaten in Alabama Riot," *New York Times*, February 19, 1965.

"I knew...until now." Lewis, p. 329.

"We was...the capitol" Williams, p. 267.

"motorcade." Branch, *Pillar of Fire*, p. 598.

"carloads...anymore." John Herbers, "Dr. King Back in Alabama, Calls for March on Capitol," *New York Times*, February 23, 1965.

"The blood...the highways." Roy Reed, "Wounded Negro Dies in Alabama," *New York Times*, February 27, 1965.

Five: Bloody Sunday

"Jimmie Lee Jackson...for caution." Lewis Menand, "The Color of Law," *New Yorker*, July 8 and 15, 2013.

"Such a march...not be tolerated." Fager, p. 89.

"We, as white…and demonstrations." Ibid.,
pp. 87–88; Williams, p. 268.

"We expected…worse than that." Lewis, p. 337.

"None of us…actually resorted." Garrow, *Protest at Selma*, p. 271, n. 82.

"There was…could hear." Lewis, p. 338.

"a sea…of them." Ibid., p. 338.

"This is…the highway." Roy Reed, "Alabama Police Use Gas and Clubs to Rout Negroes," *New York Times*, March 8, 1965.

"They spurred…and cheered." Ibid.

"The horses…unconscious." Williams, p. 269.

"The tear gas…chaotic." Vaughn, p. 140.

"A burst…fast enough." Levine, p. 128.

"In the vicious…without responsibility." Garrow, *Bearing the Cross*, pp. 399–400.

Six: Turnaround Tuesday

"the flailing clubs…fleeing blacks." Fager, p. 98.

"It looked…down on us." Williams, p. 273.

"an exercise in terror." Garrow, *Protest at Selma*, p. 81.

"a low-down…liar." Menand, "The Color of Law," *New Yorker*, July 8 and 15, 2013, p. 86.

"unusually subdued…his conscience." Garrow, *Bearing the Cross*, p. 401.

"We march…very far." Weisbrot, p. 140.

"There were…bopped this time." Gay Talese, "The Selma Walk: A Mile-Long Line," *New York Times*, March 10, 1965.

"You are ordered…have your payer." Fager, p. 104.

"All of a sudden…What's happening?" Williams, p. 274.

"Alabama's storm troopers." Weisbrot, p. 141.

"That's a kind of victory in itself." Talese, "The Selma Walk," *New York Times*, March 10, 1965.

"We love Governor…in our heart." Weisbrot, p. 141.

"We knew…retaliatory violence." Garrow, *Bearing the Cross*, p. 404.

"It is wrong…this nation." Ibid., p. 408.

"part of…*shall* overcome." May, p. 121.

"We were all…the movement." Williams, p. 278.

Seven: A Good Day to Be Alive

"When we get…the ballot." Roy Reed, "Freedom March Begins at Selma," *New York Times*, March 22, 1965.

"Communist-trained agitators." Williams, p. 279.

"Yankee trash go home" Ibid.

"This is…be alive." Adler, "Letter from Selma."

"Just got to tramp…do my part." Weisbrot, p. 145.

"The teenagers…the rest of them." Williams, p. 282.

"I was responsible…to the site." Vaughn, pp. 75–76.

"Will you march…you'll take two." Adler, "Letter from Selma."

"To me…entire nation." Lewis, p. 359.

"The racists…of happiness." Hardwick, p. 8.

"At first…vote myself." Fager, p. 155

"I came…everybody's business." Adler, "Letter from Selma."

"Make way for the originals!" Adler, "Letter from Selma."

"The marchers…almost biblical." Roy Reed, "Alabama Marchers Reach Outskirts of Montgomery," *New York Times*, March 25, 1965.

"When the marchers…how far it is." Levine, p. 120.

"We are…its conscience." Roy Reed, "25,000 Go to Alabama's Capitol," *New York Times*, March 26, 1965.

"difficult days…season of suffering." Weisbrot, p. 148.

"We *have* overcome today." Ibid.

Eight: Because They Marched

"Recent events…and speedy." Williams, p. 282.

"You know…right to vote." Ibid., p. 285.

"Today is a triumph…right to vote." E. W. Kenworthy, "Johnson Signs Voting Rights Bill, Orders Immediate Enforcement," *New York Times*, August 7, 1965.

"where past experience." Ibid.

"It is because…before you today." *CNN Late Edition with Wolf Blitzer*, March 4, 2007, http://transcripts.cnn.com/TRANSCRIPTS/0703/04/le.02.html.

Epilogue

"Our country…has made great strides." Adam Liptak, "Supreme Court Invalidates Key Part of Voting Rights Act," *New York Times*, June 25, 2013.

"disserved by today's decision." Ibid.

"deeply disappointed." Ibid.

"It is awful…Voting Rights Act of 1965." ABC News, June 25, 2013, http://abcnews.go.com/Politics/video/rep-john-lewis-scotus-decision-dagger-heart-voting-19483438.

SELECTED BIBLIOGRAPHY

The Selma voting rights campaign attracted massive national and international media coverage—a boon to future researchers. I have drawn on eyewitness press reports, on interpretive articles and essays by observers who traveled to Selma, and on interviews conducted over the years with marchers and demonstrators whose testimonies even decades later speak eloquently of the passions of the time.

Notable books that deal specifically with the Selma campaign include Gary May's *Bending Toward Justice: The Voting Rights Act and the Transformation of American Democracy*, a work cited by U.S. Supreme Court Justice Ruth Bader Ginsburg in her dissenting opinion on the Court's 2013 ruling invalidating a key provision of the Voting Rights Act; Charles E. Fager's *Selma 1965: The March That Changed the South*, informed by Fager's experiences as an activist in the voting rights campaign (he once spent a night in jail with Martin Luther King); and David J. Garrow's scholarly *Protest at Selma: Martin Luther King, Jr., and the Voting Rights Act of 1965*. Garrow is also the author of the Pulitzer Prize–winning biography *Bearing the Cross: Martin Luther King, Jr., and the Southern Christian Leadership Conference*.

The Selma Campaign 1963–1965: The Decisive Battle of the Civil Rights Movement, compiled and edited by Wally G. Vaughn and Mattie Campbell Davis, offers an invaluable collection of interviews with people from all walks of life who were involved in the voting rights campaign. *Freedom's Children: Young Civil Rights Activists Tell Their Own Stories* by Ellen Levine presents the testimonies of African Americans who were children or teenagers in the 1950s and 1960s.

Histories of the civil rights movement that I found especially informative include Taylor Branch's monumental studies *Parting the Waters: America in the King Years 1954–63*, winner of the Pulitzer Prize, and *Pillar of Fire: America in the King Years 1963–65*; Robert Weisbrot's concise *Freedom Bound: A History of America's Civil Rights Movement*; and Juan Williams's *Eyes on the Prize: America's Civil Rights Years 1954–1965*, published as a companion to the six-part PBS television series.

John Lewis's *Walking With the Wind: A Memoir of the Movement* is a compelling personal history by a battle-scarred SNCC field worker who suffered his first skull fracture as a freedom rider and his second as a leader of the Bloody Sunday march, and who has served in the U.S. Congress since 1987 as the representative for Georgia's 5th Congressional District.

Renata Adler's "Letter from Selma" is a perceptive on-the-scene report of the five-day march from Selma to Montgomery. And Elizabeth Hardwick's *Bartleby in Manhattan & Other Essays* includes an account of her visit to Selma in March 1965.

Adler, Renata. "Letter from Selma." *New Yorker*, April 10, 1965. http://www.newyorker.com/archive/1965/04/10/1965_04_10_121_TNY_CARDS_000282138.

Branch, Taylor. *Parting the Waters: America in the King Years 1954–63*. New York: Simon & Schuster, 1988.

———. *Pillar of Fire: America in the King Years 1963–65*. New York: Simon & Schuster, 1988.

Fager, Charles E. *Selma 1965: The March That Changed the South*. New York: Charles Scribner's Sons, 1974.

Garrow, David J. *Bearing the Cross: Martin Luther King, Jr., and the Southern Christian Leadership Conference*. New York: Harper Collins, 1986.

———. *Protest at Selma: Martin Luther King, Jr., and the Voting Rights Act of 1965*. New Haven: Yale University Press, 1978.

Hardwick, Elizabeth. *Bartleby in Manhattan & Other Essays.* New York: Random House, 1983.

Levine, Ellen. *Freedom's Children: Young Civil Rights Activists Tell Their Own Stories.* New York: G. P. Putnam's Sons, 1993; Puffin, 2000.

Lewis, John. *Walking With the Wind: A Memoir of the Movement.* New York: Harcourt Brace, 1998.

May, Gary. *Bending Toward Justice: The Voting Rights Act and the Transformation of American Democracy.* New York: Basic Books, 2013.

Vaughn, Wally G., and Mattie Campbell Davis, eds. *The Selma Campaign 1963–1965: The Decisive Battle of the Civil Rights Movement.* Dover, MA: Majority Press, 2006.

Weisbrot, Robert. *Freedom Bound: A History of America's Civil Rights Movement.* New York: W. W. Norton, 1990.

Williams, Juan. *Eyes on the Prize: America's Civil Rights Years 1954–1965.* New York: Penguin, 1987.

PHOTO CREDITS

INDEX

FBI, 13, 66

Fifteenth Amendment, 6

firebombings, 12–13, *12*, 17, *17*

Forman, James, 17

Fowler, James, 32

Freedom Rides, 12–13, *12*, *14*, 18, 39, 74

Gandhi, Mohandas, 13

George Washington Carver houses, 2

Ginsberg, Ruth Bader, 71

Good Samaritan Hospital, 43

Gray, Jerome, 10

Greensboro, N.C., 74

Green Street Baptist Church, 59

Hardwick, Elizabeth, 60

Hare, James A., 23

Herbers, John, 27–28

High Hope Baptist Church, *17*

Hotel Albert, 26–27, *26*, 35

House of Representatives, U.S., 67

Hudson High, 18, 20, 41

Hunter, J. D., 8

"I have a dream" speech (King), 23, 74

integration, racial, 10, 12–13
    see also segregation

Jackson, Jimmie Lee, 32–33, 34, *34*, 56, 75

Javits, Jacob, 45

Jim Crow laws, 9, 13

Johnson, Frank M., Jr., 45, 47, 53

Johnson, Lyndon B., 2, 31, 34, 51, 54, 60, 67,
    68, 69, 75

Justice Department, U.S., 13, 35, 47

King, Martin Luther, Jr., vii, 23, 24, *25*, 26–27,
    26, 28, 34, 35, *36*, 51, 53, 66, 67, *68*, 71,
    74
  arrests of, 29, *29*
  assassination of, 69, 75
  Selma-to-Montgomery marches and, 33, 36,
    44, 45, 46–47, *46*, 47, 49, 51, *52*, 56, 60,
    62, 65, *65*

Ku Klux Klan, 8, *8*, 59, 65–66, *66*

Lafayette, Bernard, 13, *14*, 15–16, 18

Lafayette, Colia, 13, 15, 16

Lee, Cager, 32, 56, 69

Lee, Viola, 32

Leoline, Sister Mary, 56

Letherer, James, 56, *57*

"Letter from a Birmingham Jail" (King),
    29

"Letter from a Selma Jail" (King), 29

Lewis, John, vii, 22–23, 32, 35–36, *36*, 39, *40*,
    60, 71–72

Lincoln, Abraham, 69

Lingo, Colonel, 35, 39

literacy tests, 6, 8, 22, 69

Liuzzo, Viola, 65–66, *66*

Lowndes County, 59

McClain, H. C., *17*

Manuel, Johnny, 20

March on Washington (1963), 23, 74

Marion, Ala., 32, 33, 34

Marshall, Thurgood, 75

mass arrests, 20–21, 29, 31, 36, 56

Montgomery, Ala., 10, 13, 65
    see also Selma-to-Montgomery marches

Montgomery bus boycott, 10, 23, 74

Moore, Margaret, 41

Morton, Bernice, 8, 59

Moton, Leroy, 59, 65–66

movie theaters, segregated, 9, 10, 11

National Guard, U.S., 54

National States Rights Party, 27

Newberry's, 9

New York Times, 28, 39, 47, 62

Nobel Peace Prize, 23, 74

nonviolent resistance, 13, 18, 28, 29, 43

Obama, Barack, 70, 71

Parks, Rosa, 10, 67, 74

Perkins, James, Jr., 70

Peter, Paul, and Mary, 62

Philadelphia, Miss., 8

Pickard, J. A., 2

police riots, 32

poll taxes, 6, 69

protest marches, 18, 28–29, 51